CUSTOMER SERVICE Rules!

CUSTOMER SERVICE Rules!

52 ways to create a customer-centric business

written by **DON GALLEGOS**

illustrated by **STEVE HICKNER**

BRIGANTINE MEDIA

Customer Service Rules! Copyright © 2014 by Don Gallegos and Brigantine Media. All rights reserved. No part of this book may be reproduced or utilized in any way or by any means, electronic or mechanical, including photocopying, recording, or any information storage or retrieval system without permission in writing from the publisher.

Illustrations by Steve Hickner

Brigantine Media
211 North Avenue, St. Johnsbury, Vermont 05819
Phone: 802-751-8802 | Fax: 802-751-8804
Email: neil@brigantinemedia.com
Website: www.brigantinemedia.com

ISBN 978-1-9384063-9-3

Dedication

To Our Lord who has blessed me with my beautiful wife, Cheri, and our six children, Tresa, Paul, David, Jerry, Ann Marie, and Mary Lynn. I am eternally grateful.

Acknowledgments

Thanks to my parents who provided an excellent Jesuit education for me, and a father who reminded me that "there will always be people smarter than you and people dumber than you, but you can always outwork all of them."

Thanks to the mentors I have worked with along the way, Lloyd King and Ray Rose, and the wonderful employees at King Soopers who were all an inspiration for me.

The Rules

PART ONE: CUSTOMERS

1	The customer is not always right.	3
2	Don't ask for the receipt.	5
3	Let customers bring back an item you don't stock.	6
4	A store credit is not a refund.	8
5	Give more refund than the customer expects.	10
6	Don't let accountants make customer service policy.	11
7	Eliminate re-stocking fees.	13
8	Agree with the customer.	14
9	A "jerk" is a customer, too.	15
10	Don't embarrass a customer.	17
11	Welcome customer complaints.	19
12	Say "thank you" sincerely.	21
13	Don't ask for unnecessary information.	23
14	Don't make your problem the customer's problem.	25
15	Admit your mistakes. Right away.	27
16	Do what you advertise.	29
17	Don't do less than you advertise.	31
18	Customer service is not a department.	33
19	Use the customer's name.	35
20	Talk to your customers.	37
21	Acknowledge the customer.	39
22	Compassion makes a difference.	40
23	Treat customers as guests.	42
24	Have you found everything today?	43
25	Be flexible.	44
26	Stock special requests.	46
27	Take care of the customer, part 1.	48
28	Take care of the customer, part 2.	50

The Rules

PART TWO: EMPLOYEES

29 Treat employees with respect. 55
30 Treat employees as valuable customers. 56
31 Empower your employees. 58
32 Don't hide behind Mr. Policy. 60
33 Give employees the tools to deal with customer complaints. 61
34 No mystery shoppers. 63
35 Look for a great attitude. 64
36 Help people instead of judging them. 65
37 Love it or leave it. 67
38 Penny wise can mean pound foolish. 69

PART THREE: MANAGEMENT

39 Learn from top service companies. 73
40 Great customer service costs money. 75
41 Customer service training should never stop. 77
42 Hold regular customer service meetings. 78
43 Go for written comments, not numbers. 79
44 Take every customer comment seriously. 81
45 Monitor your customer service successes and failures. 83
46 Make every employee part of the customer service team. 84
47 ROI = Return On Individual. 86
48 The CEO must spend time with employees. 87
49 Know the value of a customer. 89
50 Serve your community. 90
51 Recognize your employees. 91
52 Walk the talk. 92

INTRODUCTION

I WAS FORTUNATE in my career to have worked for two different retail supermarket chains. The first was Miller's Supermarket in Denver, where I worked for ten years as a grocery buyer. I was trained there and learned the basics of dealing with customers.

But my real education in customer service started when I had the opportunity to work for King Soopers, which was a fifteen-store regional chain when I first began work there. I learned how vital customer service is to any business from the founder, Lloyd King.

Here are a couple of examples of Lloyd King's philosophy of handling customers and employees:

- Shortly after starting work at King Soopers, King sent me a note to let me know that he was adjusting my vacation. Normally, an employee received one week of vacation after one year of working at the company. But since I had worked ten years for Miller's, he was giving me two weeks. I thought, "Wow! He didn't have to do that, but he did, without my asking!"

- I searched for a discontinued product on behalf of a customer who wanted to send it to her son in the military. I found the last case from the broker and had it shipped to her at no charge. When King found out what I had done, he sent me a note to tell me that he appreciated the way I had handled the request. The note said: "This is the way we like to treat customers."

I still have that handwritten note.

Our culture at King Soopers when I was president was to give superior customer service. Not just good—*superior*. When a customer complained that his DVD rented from our store broke his television set, we paid to have the set fixed, even though the repairman said the DVD wasn't the problem. My philosophy of customer service is to win the customer, not the argument.

I'm convinced that people don't really know what superior service is until they get it. I believe that our superior customer service helped King Soopers thrive as other chains went out of business. Throughout this book, you'll read more stories about exceptional customer service that you can use to guide the way your business handles customers.

PART 1
Customers

RULE
1

The customer is not always right.

WE'VE HEARD IT over and over—"The customer is always right." Guess what? The customer is NOT always right—but he or she is always the customer.

Employees want to protect the company and they don't want to let a customer "get away" with anything. They spend too much time thinking about who is right and who is wrong in a situation.

When they tell me the customer is wrong, I say, "So what? Just take care of the customer and move on."

Our supermarkets rented videos and we charged a late fee if the customer was late bringing back a tape. I received a letter from a customer who said his children had rented two videos, but he and his wife didn't realize that they had done so. He asked the head clerk at the store if she could she do anything about the ten dollar charge, because it wasn't his fault.

The head clerk, thinking she was doing a good job of providing customer service, said, "How about five dollars?" This made the customer even angrier, and prompted his letter to the president about how cheap we were. The next day, the manager went to the customer's house with five dollars and a gift certificate as an apology to being so insensitive to his problem.

I explained to the clerk that we don't make money on late charges—we make money renting videos. "When a customer brings back a video, be happy. Now we can rent it again. Even though the customer is wrong and he does owe ten dollars, he's mad. When a customer is obviously mad about late charges, waive the charge—not all late charges, just when the customer is mad. We want him to keep shopping with us."

The goal is to win the *customer*—<u>not</u> the argument.

RULE 2

Don't ask for the receipt.

MOST COMPANIES WANT a receipt for an item a customer brings back for a refund. I don't think that is necessary.

It doesn't really matter when the customer bought the item, or even if the customer bought the item somewhere else. If *you* give the customer the money back, you've gained that customer for life.

Sure, a few customers will take advantage, but ninety-eight percent of customers are honest. Why have a policy to "catch" the two percent of cheaters? A customer will be delighted to buy from you, knowing that they can return anything with no questions asked.

The end result when you don't ask for the receipt—more business and more profit.

RULE 3

Let customers bring back an item you don't stock.

IF A CUSTOMER brings back an item you don't stock, don't send them back to the store where they originally purchased it. Take back the item, give the refund, and keep the customer in *your* store.

After you give the refund, you can take it back to the store where they originally purchased the item, or put it on your shelf and sell it.

A customer came to the courtesy desk of King Soopers and set down a carton of milk that was Safeway's private label. Immediately, the customer realized she wasn't in Safeway and said, "I'm sorry, I'm in the wrong store." The clerk asked what was wrong with the milk. The customer replied, "It's sour—but it's Safeway's milk." The clerk said, "That's okay, just go back and help yourself to one of ours."

Now, <u>that</u> is a clerk who understands customer service! And you can bet the customer told all her friends about it.

RULE 4

A store credit is not a refund.

I WAS SHOPPING at a lovely clothing store for a gift for my wife. I had about four hundred dollars worth of clothes on the counter. As the clerk was ringing it up, I noticed a sign that said, "Refunds are for store credit only." I asked the clerk, "If my wife doesn't like what I purchased, she can't get a refund, only a store credit?" The clerk said, "Yes, that is our policy." I told her to tear up the charge—I didn't want the items I just purchased.

If she didn't like what I chose, there might not have been something else in the store that she wanted. It's hard to understand why some businesses have such anti-customer policies. When you make a company policy, first think: "Will this work for the customer?"

PS: That exclusive dress shop is now out of business. And they earned it.

RULE 5

Give more refund than the customer expects.

WITH A REFUND or exchange, customers rarely ask for more than a company is willing to give them. People want satisfaction. That's the goal of a refund or an exchange.

Give the customer a little more than she asks for. If a customer wants to exchange a product, give her the product she wants, and add a small gift certificate as an apology for her inconvenience.

She won't expect it, and she'll be delighted with the outcome of the transaction. It will set you apart from your competition.

RULE 6

Don't let accountants make customer service policy.

SOME POLICIES SEEM to be written to punish customers. Have you ever noticed that some companies print their refund policy on sales receipts? It's usually complicated and in very small type.

At one department store I shopped at, the refund policy listed all the things you must do when bringing back a product: You had to return it in the original box with the wrapping. You couldn't return it after thirty days. In other words: Don't you dare bring this back.

Most companies give the authority to write refund policies to the accounting department. That's wrong-headed. The accounting department should keep track of the numbers, but it should not make marketing decisions.

The financial officer in our company asked me one day, "Do you want to see how much our refund policy is costing us?" I said, "No." He said, "It's a big number." I said, "Yes, but so is our profit. It's an even bigger number."

Our simple refund policy contributed to, rather than subtracted from, our bottom line.

RULE 7

Eliminate re-stocking fees.

WHAT MISGUIDED ACCOUNTANT came up with the idea of a re-stocking fee? When customers bring back items they don't want, an organization that charges a re-stocking fee will just generate more bad will.

There is a cost to re-stocking, but that is part of the cost of doing business, and it is already built in to your margins. Too many organizations spend time thinking up these so-called solutions to lowering their operating expenses. They are squandering their most valuable commodity—customer loyalty.

If the purpose of a re-stocking fee is to make customers keep items they don't want, that is a sure way to help a company go out of business.

RULE 8

Agree with the customer.

WHEN A CUSTOMER is upset, the first thing to do is agree with the customer. Tell the customer you are surprised he or she isn't madder.

Murray Raphel, a clothing retailer and leading marketer, used to tell irate customers, "Okay, you have two choices. I'll either refund your money immediately or I'll give you a store credit. Which would you prefer?"

When a customer is really mad and you agree with the customer, you immediately de-escalate the situation.

You can gain a customer for life when you kill 'em with kindness.

RULE 9

A "jerk" is a customer, too.

SOMETIMES YOU CAN get a customer who is a real "jerk." But the "jerk" spends money with you (see Rule 1). You need to treat the "jerk" with great respect.

The "jerk" is probably being treated badly everywhere he shops, because he's a "jerk" to everyone. So you have an opportunity to get all his business.

We had a "jerk" who called ahead and wanted his pharmacy prescription ready as soon as he came into the store. The clerks made him wait in line as they filled orders before his, and he became irate. When I investigated the situation, I found that the so-called "jerk" spent one thousand dollars a month with us. To my mind, this "jerk" was one of our most valuable customers.

I told our pharmacy staff to always have this

customer's prescription ready when he came into the store.

The "jerk" is not going to change—*you* have to change. Teach employees that most people don't behave like the "jerk," so, for him, you'll make an exception.

Never let a "jerk" know you think he is a "jerk."

RULE 10

Don't embarrass a customer.

WHEN A CUSTOMER approaches you with a problem, don't embarrass the customer.

Stew Leonard, a supermarket owner, recalled a situation early in his career when a customer brought back a quart of milk. The customer said the milk was sour. Stew smelled the milk, and pronounced it not sour. Stew then called over the dairy manager, who sniffed the carton and also said the milk was fine. Stew told the customer that even though they thought the milk wasn't sour, he would give her credit for the quart of milk.

The customer was embarrassed by all this sniffing, and said she would never shop there again.

Stew said it was a tremendous lesson. "Why

would I tell her it wasn't sour if I was going to give her money back anyway? I refunded her money and still lost the customer!"

He vowed to try to never embarrass a customer again.

RULE
11

Welcome customer complaints.

WHEN A CUSTOMER tells you she is dissatisfied, she is doing your company a real service.

Think about it for a minute.

If the customer doesn't complain, she will go home mad. Angry customers tell thirteen people, on average, about their bad experience. Happy customers tell seven people how well they were treated.

You want the odds on *your* side.

If a customer tells you she is unhappy, she is giving you an opportunity to fix the problem. And if you do a good job satisfying unhappy customers, the customers will praise your store rather than complain about your service.

If one customer complains to you, there are probably others with the same problem who aren't speaking up.

Welcome complaints. The complaining customer is your best friend.

RULE 12

Say "thank you" sincerely.

IT'S VERY IMPORTANT to remember to say "thank you." But it's even more important to say it sincerely.

Author Harvey Mackay wrote, "'Thank you' should be part of everyone's vocabulary."

The CEO should say "thank you" when employees do something extra to help the company. A written thank you note from the CEO will make an employee feel like a million dollars.

Employees need to be trained to make "thank you" a meaningful phrase. They must learn that without customers there are no sales, and no sales means the company is out of business.

A sincere "thank you" may be the most important two words any employee—at any level—can say.

RULE 13

Don't ask for unnecessary information.

HAVE YOU EVER used your credit card in a store, and then the clerk asked to see your driver's license?

This has happened to me far too many times. When I ask why, they always say (of course), "It's our policy." But I've wondered: What if I didn't have a driver's license? Could I still buy this?

I purchased some gift cards at a department store and the clerk asked for my phone number. I asked her, "Why do you need a phone number?" She replied that it was for my protection if my credit card was stolen.

But that is not true. It is not for my protection. It is not Visa's policy to ask for my phone number. If my card is stolen, that is Visa's problem. I don't need the Big Brother of a store protecting me from myself.

Unnecessary information is intrusive and has great potential to embarrass customers. Decide what you need to know to get the job done, and don't ask customers to supply more information.

RULE
14

Don't make your problem the customer's problem.

PEOPLE ARE SO used to lousy service they really don't know good customer service until they get it. They often accept bad service because they think that's the way it's supposed to be.

Customers often take the consequences of events over which they have no control. A prime example of this is a situation I encountered a few years ago with Ticketmaster.

We all know that when you order tickets for a concert or other event, Ticketmaster charges a handling fee for getting you the ticket. Fine.

But on rare occasions, they sell tickets to a concert that gets cancelled. On this occasion, Ticketmaster refunded the money, but not the fee for handling. Apparently the company felt that just giving the customer back the cost of the ticket was "good enough." They made over $35,000 from the fees alone.

But that was wrong. Ticketmaster was making *its* problem *my* problem. I had no control over whether the concert would be held. Ticketmaster takes that as a risk of doing business. If I couldn't go to the concert, the fair thing was to refund the entire cost of the transaction.

Plenty of people would accept that Ticketmaster was entitled to their handling charge, but I disagree. When you are committed to providing excellent customer service, don't pass your problems on to your customers. They will be pleasantly surprised by your seemingly generous practice and thank you for it.

RULE
15

Admit your mistakes. Right away.

IN 1982, SOMEONE laced several bottles of Tylenol with cyanide and seven people died as a result. Johnson & Johnson acted quickly and ordered all Tylenol recalled from every outlet in the country, not just those in the Chicago area where the deaths occurred. The company decided not to reissue the product until they developed tamperproof packaging that would make it much more difficult for a similar incident to occur in the future. The cost was high, but within five months of the disaster, the company had recovered seventy percent of its market share for the drug. Many consumers were so reassured that they switched from other painkillers to Tylenol.

When the recall occurred, our company ran an ad that said to bring back the recalled product, regardless where you purchased it, and we would refund your money, no receipt required. But we were just about the only store to do this. Everyone else wanted that receipt to give the refund.

But it was only common sense for us to act this way. Johnson & Johnson was giving us full credit for all the Tylenol we returned to them, so we were not losing any money.

It wasn't rocket science to handle the recall this way—just using good judgment that possibly gained some new customers who might not have shopped with us before.

RULE 16

Do what you advertise.

WHEN YOU SAY you will do something, you'd better do it.

My wife and I went to a restaurant on Valentine's Day. I had made my reservation thirty days before. When we arrived at the reserved time, the hostess said, "It'll be a forty-five minute wait for your table." I asked why there was such a long wait. She said, "Well, you know it's Valentine's Day."

Not the best answer. I said, "Yes, I know it's Valentine's Day. It happens every February 14th."

Obviously, the restaurant over-booked in case people canceled at the last minute. That is ridiculous. Cancellations are part of the restaurant business, and you can fill the cancellations with walk-ins. When a restaurant takes reservations, they can't operate in a way that shows customers they didn't mean it.

When a store advertises it will have a certain product, make sure there's enough inventory to cover the demand. Do what you say you will do.

RULE 17

Don't do less than you advertise.

A FEW YEARS ago, Blockbuster announced that there would no longer be late fees on rentals. They were competing with Netflix, which did not have late fees regardless how long you kept the DVD.

The problem: Blockbuster's announcement was not true. If you rented from them you had to give your credit card. If you kept the movie past seven days, they charged your credit card the full retail price of the DVD.

Customers complained so much that Blockbuster had to refund the charges to customers and pay $630,000 to settle legal claims with almost every state. A spokesperson for Blockbuster admitted that the signage in the stores needed to explain the "fine print" of the program better.

And we all know the end to this story: Blockbuster is out of business.

RULE 18

Customer service is not a department.

LEE COCKERELL, FORMER executive vice president of Walt Disney World, said, "Customer service is not a department."

I was in the habit of renting a car from the "We try harder" rental car company once a quarter when I attended board meetings in Wisconsin. On one trip, I picked up the car at the airport and drove the four miles to my hotel for the night without any problem. The next morning, I went out to start the car, but the battery was dead.

I called Avis and explained the problem. The customer representative said, "We will bring you another car." I replied, "I don't have time for that. Just pick up the car at the hotel. The keys are at the check-in desk." I took a cab to my meeting, and later to the airport, and flew home.

Avis charged me for the car.

I tried calling the president of Avis, but I ended up with a clerk in the "customer service department." She said, "Mr. Gallegos, you drove the car and had it overnight." I told her I drove the car a total of four miles before it broke down. She apologized, but said she couldn't change the company's policy.

Then I wrote the president a letter. The following week I received a letter from Avis saying they were sorry, and enclosed two fifty-dollar gift certificates to use the next time I rented a car from them.

Now that's arrogant—what would make them think I would ever rent from Avis again? It's not the only rent-a-car company in business.

I sent the gift certificates back and included a copy of my book, *Win the Customer, Not the Argument*, in hopes they would learn a little about real customer service. I had been renting four times a year from Avis for nine years, but I never rented from them again.

Customer service means helping your customer—it's not just the name of a department.

RULE
19

Use the customer's name.

TEACH EMPLOYEES TO go out of their way to get the customer's name so they can address them directly. People feel great when they go into a store and the associate says, "Hi, Don" or "Hi, Mary." It's powerful.

Here are a few easy ways to learn customers' names:

- When an employee sees a customer shopping, approach the customer and say, "Hi, I'm Joe—thank you so much for shopping with us. Can I help you find anything? What's your name?"

- When the customer pays by check or credit card, the customer's name is right there. Always thank the customer using his/her name.
- If your business has a loyalty program, the computer system will bring up the customer's name when the card is scanned, and the employee can thank the customer using his/her name.

If every employee learned one name a day, how many customers would your store get to know in a week or a month?

RULE 20

Talk to your customers.

COMPUTERIZED SYSTEMS THAT answer phone calls have their place—like phoning in to renew a prescription, which is quick and easy, and you really don't need to talk with anyone to get the job done. But voice mail really irritates people. When you have to push different numbers to get the right department, the first choice should be: "If you want to talk with someone, press *one*." Usually, it's the last option.

Our company always had a person answer the phone. It's the polite thing to do, and people couldn't believe they actually got a real live person on the phone right away.

When I was president, I always answered my own phone. If an irate customer who wanted to talk to the president called and actually got me, then I was already ahead of the game. Customers were so surprised to hear my voice and learn that they were talking with the president that they often forgot their complaint! If I wasn't in my office, my assistant found me when an irate customer called. If a customer was really mad, I wanted to take that call.

That's one way to find out if something is going wrong in one of your stores—by talking with the customers.

RULE
21

Acknowledge the customer.

WHEN YOU ARE busy with a customer and another one comes in your area, always acknowledge the customer by saying "Hello, I'll be with you shortly." The customer will feel good about being noticed. And when you are finished with the previous customer, say, " I appreciate you waiting—now, what can I help you with?"

Discount Tire is a master at this. When there is a line, the employee always says, "Hello, I'll be with you shortly." And when they are ready to wait on you, they come out from behind the counter to greet you.

It is a small thing, but customers really appreciate the recognition.

RULE 22

Compassion makes a difference.

GIVING GOOD CUSTOMER service can have repercussions far beyond the original encounter between employee and customer.

Sometimes a customer is in a bad mood. The employee's job is to remember that people have difficulties sometimes. An employee can make a customer's day by being extremely nice to everyone.

Just a pleasant question such as, "Is there anything else I can do for you today?" makes the customer feel that you care. Make sure your employees say something like, "Thanks for shopping with us today," in a friendly voice. Little forms of encouragement can make all the difference to customers. And when a customer has a real problem, the employee should try to solve it immediately.

The employee might change that customer's

attitude. After handling a customer service issue, people have told me, "You changed my life."

It's amazing what you can accomplish by just being nice.

RULE
23

Treat customers as guests.

CHANGE YOUR WHOLE approach to customer service and address your customers as "guests." It is a small thing, but it sends an important message.

We all like to be treated as guests.

RULE 24

Have you found everything today?

TEACH EMPLOYEES, PARTICULARLY checkout clerks, to always ask the customer, "Have you found everything today?" It's amazing to discover how often customers can't find something, but since they are in a hurry, they just go to the checkout with the rest of their items. On ten thousand customers a week, increasing the average sale by fifty cents amounts to five thousand dollars in sales.

Help customers find what they want to buy!

RULE
25

Be flexible.

OUR STORES WERE open from 7:00 a.m. to 11:00 p.m. One night at five minutes before 11:00, a customer jumped out of his car to run into the store before it closed. A clerk inside the store ran to get the door locked—and the clerk won.

What would have happened if the clerk had allowed the customer to come in? The customer would have bought some things, then the clerk would have rung up the sale, and then bag the groceries. Wow! This could have been a lot of trouble!

It wasn't the clerk's fault. He was told to close at 11:00 p.m. No one ever said, "Be a little flexible."

We solved the problem by opening fifteen minutes early, at 6:45 a.m., and closing fifteen minutes late, at 11:15 p.m. Customers loved it. It's great to get to a store a few minutes early and find that it's already open. It's especially nice when you are rushing to get to the store before it closes and you are a few minutes late, but they are still open.

This small customer service can create a lot of good feelings.

RULE
26

Stock special requests.

ALWAYS TRY TO do what nobody else will do. You can never go too far to please a customer.

If a customer requests an item you don't stock, let the customer know you will be happy to order the product and notify the customer when it comes in.

One of our best customers wanted a competitor's private label dog food. Obviously, we didn't stock a competitor's private label product. But I didn't want that customer to have to go to our competitor for the dog food.

The manager went to the competitor's store, bought a case of the dog food, and put it in his office. He called the customer to let her know that whenever she wanted to buy the dog food, it was in his office, and, "by the way, it's cheaper here."

Now that's a special order!

Remember, if you send the customer to the competitor to buy one product, they won't leave with just one product. Keep your customers shopping with you.

RULE 27

Take care of the customer, part 1.

FIFTEEN YEARS AGO we operated our own photo labs for our supermarkets. It was a necessary customer service that was also profitable.

A customer who had taken pictures of dental equipment that he was selling brought the film to our store to be developed. In the meantime, he shipped the dental equipment from Denver to Southern California. He came in on a Monday to pick up the film and we could not find it. The customer was upset. He needed the pictures to show to his client the next morning. So we told him we would do everything possible to get his pictures. And that's what we did.

We checked all our stores and couldn't find the pictures.

The photo lab manager called the customer and found out where he shipped the dental equipment—Long Beach, California.

It just happened that the manager's sister lived in Long Beach. He phoned her and had her hire a photographer to take pictures of the dental equipment. She mailed the roll of film by flying it ticket counter to ticket counter to Denver—all in the same day. The film arrived that evening at 10:00 p.m. The photo lab manager picked it up, developed the film, and had it delivered to the customer before his meeting on Tuesday.

Wow! What service!

It's important to recognize the customer shouldn't care what we have to do to get him his pictures. He didn't lose them. *We* did.

PS: Our photo lab manager knew what to do. He didn't even have to call his supervisor, because he was trained to "do what it takes" to take care of customers.

RULE 28

Take care of the customer, part 2.

I WROTE THIS story in my book, *Win the Customer, Not the Argument*," and I think it is worth repeating. It's an incredible example of how far employees will go if they know they can't get in trouble when they are trying to take care of the customer.

I received a letter from a father who wanted me to know how well our employees handled a situation. His daughter had been invited to her very first high school dance, but the night before the dance, her date cancelled the date. She was devastated. The next day, the dad came to our store. He told the floral department manager what had happened and asked for something nice for his daughter. The floral department manager did more than that.

The floral department manager called the house a little while later and said, "We have a courtesy clerk here who goes to the same high school your daughter does. He would be delighted to take your daughter to the dance." She was thrilled, and arrangements were made. But the floral department went even further. The employees took up a collection at the store and bought her a corsage and paid for the couple's dinner that night.

I almost fell off my chair when I read this letter, and even I thought, "Who would think to do that?"

This happened in our highest volume store on a busy Saturday, and yet they took the time to take care of a bad situation for someone they didn't even know. Do you think that dad will ever shop anywhere else?

When you create a climate for employees to do what is right, they will surprise you with what they do.

PART 2
Employees

RULE 29

Treat employees with respect.

YOU HAVE TO teach employees by your example—and you have to mean it, not fake it.

When I became president of our company, there were special parking spots in the lots marked "Reserved" for the president, vice president, and other top executives. I met with the executive committee and told them we were going to paint over the words "Reserved" so that any of our staff could park anywhere in the lot.

The next morning, an accounting clerk parked in the previously "Reserved" parking spot and told me, "Thanks. I feel like an executive."

It was a small way to send an important message of respect for everyone in the organization.

RULE
30

Treat employees as valuable customers.

TOM HAGGAI, FORMER CEO of IGA Supermarkets, says, "Your most valuable customers are your employees." Your employees interact with customers every day, and if they aren't happy with their jobs, customers won't be happy with your store.

Haggai has followed his own advice. When he was appointed CEO of IGA Supermarkets, Haggai was living in High Point, North Carolina. The IGA corporate offices were in Chicago. The IGA board of directors offered to move the corporate headquarters to North Carolina. Tom refused.

He said, "Why should I displace fifty families to make life easier for me?" Every week Tom flew to Chicago during the week and then flew back to North Carolina on the weekend.

Haggai made life hard for himself rather than his employees. His attitude about service set the example for the company.

RULE 31

Empower your employees.

TRAIN EMPLOYEES TO do what it takes to take care of the customer on the spot. When they have to call a supervisor to approve a transaction, you're paying two salaries to get one thing done.

I went into a national drug store chain to return a five dollar item. I had to wait ten extra minutes while the clerk called for a manager to approve the return. Meantime, the line behind me was growing and everyone was getting impatient. Why couldn't the chain empower its clerks to approve a five dollar return? It would save everyone's time.

Be reasonable about what you empower employees to do, and set a limit that feels right for your organization.

What if an empowered employee makes a mistake when trying to handle a customer issue? Face it—they are probably making them now, with all the policies in place that tie their hands. Be happy that they take care of the customer.

Mistakes happen. I would rather have an employee make a mistake in favor of the customer instead of the company.

RULE 32

Don't hide behind Mr. Policy.

DON'T LET EMPLOYEES hide behind a policy shield: "I would be happy to take care of this for you but it's against our policy." When I hear this, I always want to say, "Can I talk to Mr. Policy?"

But employees are just doing what they are trained to do. Policies should only be guidelines, and employees should have the flexibility to do what it takes to satisfy customers.

Write this line at the end of your policy manual: "When the situation requires it, go outside this policy." When store policies are too strict, customers with a complaint can feel unwanted.

And remember, you can't possibly have a policy that covers *every* situation.

RULE
33

Give employees the tools to deal with customer complaints.

WHEN YOU EMPOWER employees to handle customer problems, you also have to help them know what to do.

We gave every employee a booklet of gift certificates, each good for a half-gallon of ice cream or a free video rental. All employees carried a booklet with them at all times. We trained our employees to give a customer a gift certificate as an apology when they encountered a problem.

Even a customer who helped to bag her own groceries would be handed a certificate as our way of apologizing for being short of help.

The gift certificate gave the employee an easy way to clear up small issues, and customers were always delighted to receive one.

RULE
34

No mystery shoppers.

MANY ORGANIZATIONS HIRE mystery shoppers who go around and check on the employees to see if they are treating customers according to the organization's philosophy. I think this stinks.

I don't think it's fair to the employees, and it sends a message that you don't trust them.

If you are serious about monitoring customer comment cards, you don't need to hire an outside agency to give you the information you are already getting from real customers.

Ban the mystery shoppers! Use your *actual* shoppers to track your customer service instead.

RULE 35

Look for a great attitude.

WHEN HIRING EMPLOYEES, it's important to determine if they have a good attitude. Not everyone can deal with customers. An employee who has a bad attitude will never give good customer service.

Many employees are in the wrong job, and it's not their fault. Someone hired them and put them in the job they aren't right for.

When you are hiring people whose job it is to handle customers day in and day out, you have to hire people who like to smile. Not a forced smile, a genuine smile.

Feargal Quinn, a great Irish businessman and politician, said that when he interviewed front line employees, he didn't pay much attention to what the job candidate said. He just kept track of how much they smiled. He hired the candidates who smiled the most!

RULE
36

Help people instead of judging them.

WE ALL HAVE a tendency to judge people by their appearance. That's a really bad practice when it comes to customer service.

A truck driver who parked in a lot near his bank had a ticket for the bank to validate so he would not have to pay the parking fee. He finished his transaction and went back to his truck, but realized he forgot to have the teller stamp his parking ticket. He returned to the bank, but the teller who had waited on him had left for a break, so he went to another teller and asked her to stamp the ticket.

The new teller said she couldn't stamp it, because she hadn't waited on him. The driver said he had just finished a transaction at the bank five minutes earlier.

He asked to see a bank vice president. The truck driver told the vice president that he was withdrawing all the money in his account. He said, "I'm taking my money to a bank that wants my business."

He withdrew one and a half million dollars—over a parking stamp—and went down the street to another bank to redeposit the money. The driver wasn't dressed like a Wall Street tycoon, but he had the bank account of one.

Don't judge people, help people—it's more fun.

RULE 37

Love it or leave it.

I PITY THE people who go to work every day and hate their jobs.

When I speak to groups, people sometimes tell me after the speech, "I have a boss who is awful. He won't let me provide the kind of customer service you're talking about."

I respond this way: "We all have had good bosses and bad bosses. When you have a bad boss, do everything you can to get your boss promoted, and then you'll get a new one." In other words, do your job as well as you can. Don't stand around complaining, because then you won't give good customer service. If you are always complaining, it is infectious to everyone around you.

DON GALLEGOS

When employees are unhappy, customers will pick up a negative vibe, either because of the employee's attitude or because customers hear the employee complaining to co-workers. Unhappy employees are like a disease that must be cured or the whole company will be infected.

My advice to unhappy employees: If after trying hard for a couple of months, you still don't like your job, get out. Life is too short to be working and complaining.

RULE
38

Penny wise can mean pound foolish.

YOU PROBABLY READ about the woman who bought a cup of coffee at McDonald's and it spilled on her. The coffee burned her so badly she had to go to the hospital. She wanted McDonald's to pay $20,000—the medical expenses plus her loss of income.

The company offered $800, saying she should have known the coffee was hot and it was her fault she spilled it. That may be true, but the way that McDonald's handled the problem escalated the costs tremendously.

The end of the story: She sued McDonald's and

won a major cash settlement (undisclosed but probably a little less than $600,000).

McDonald's handled this problem as a product liability issue. I've often thought Ray Kroc, longtime owner of McDonald's, was turning over in his grave with that attitude.

McDonald's would have been much better off if they treated the problem as a customer service issue and had paid her bills as she originally asked.

At King Soopers, people would ask us to pay for dents in their cars if a shopping cart hit them. Most of the time, we would pay for the damage, unless it was obvious it was not a shopping cart dent. We considered shopping cart dents a customer service problem and treated them as such, so they didn't escalate into big lawsuits. I always thought, "It's peanuts in the scheme of things."

Think about potential liability cases as customer service issues first. You'll probably save money in the long run.

PART 3
Management

RULE
39

Learn from top service companies.

STUDY ORGANIZATIONS THAT are known for their exceptional customer service.

Some years ago, I read that the Ritz-Carlton hotel in Boston won the Malcolm Baldrige National Quality Award for great customer service. I asked if I could visit with them to learn about their policies that created that success. They agreed. I found their service policies quite compelling.

Every employee at the hotel has the authority to take care of a guest problem up to $2,400. If a guest has a problem, it's dealt with quickly. But they go further. Management makes every employee aware that the guest had a problem, so that when employees see the guest in the hallway, they will offer an apology for what happened.

Here's an example from the *Wall Street Journal*

of how the Ritz-Carlton does customer service: One guest decided to stay longer, and when another guest with a reservation showed up, there was no room available. The Ritz booked the guests at a comparable hotel, sent them in a limousine to that hotel and had champagne served in the limo as they were being transported. Then the Ritz paid for their room.

That kind of customer service keeps customers forever. (It also made for great publicity.)

RULE 40

Great customer service costs money.

YOU CAN'T HAVE superior service unless you are willing to spend the money to train employees how to treat customers better than other companies do.

Hold training classes regularly and use real-life examples of customer service issues, both good and bad, so employees can relate to them. Use role playing so employees can practice what to do in every situation.

We did this at King Soopers, and our stores had the largest market share in our area because of our great customer service.

From time to time, food operators from other locations would visit to tour our stores. One day one of the executives from out of state asked me, "Why do you do so much more business than Safeway, right across the street? Your prices are the same as theirs."

I said, "Because our service is better."

I don't know of any company that went out of business because it gave superior service.

RULE
41

Customer service training should never stop.

DON'T THINK YOU have trained employees how to handle customers by having them attend a two- or three-day training class. You have to follow up when they go back to the store. Don't assume they have already been trained.

There isn't a day that goes by that a customer doesn't give you a good suggestion, or shows how they want to be served. These are all opportunities to train employees.

We can never stop learning, because every situation is different, and employees need to know how to handle them.

RULE 42

Hold regular customer service meetings.

IF YOU ARE committed to providing excellent customer service, you must hold regular meetings with all employees, with the main topic being customer service. And the president of the company should lead the meeting to show how important the topic is to the success of the company.

With 15,000 employees, once a quarter we had a meeting with twenty-five percent of the employees. It would take eight or nine meetings to reach everyone, and scheduling that many meetings was costly to the organization. But the payback from those meetings was having the employees learn how serious we were about providing superior customer service.

RULE

43

Go for written comments, not numbers.

MOST COMMENT CARDS have small boxes to check. "On a scale of 1 to 10, 10 being the best, rate our service in certain areas."

But what do those numbers really mean?

Unless the customer gives their comments in actual words, you really have nothing to use to improve your service.

When a customer has a chance to write real words, you'll often get great ideas to change your operation for the better. You can't have too many great ideas. Plus, if you change something that was suggested and the customer knows it was due to his/her suggestion, guess how many people he/she will tell.

The president of the company can read a

percentage of the comment cards and three or four top people in the organization can each read a percentage of the comment cards.

When one customer gives you a suggestion, don't assume it is just one customer comment. It's likely there are many others who feel the same way.

RULE
44

Take every customer comment seriously.

CUSTOMER COMMENTS CAN reveal more than simple mistakes.

A high school teacher asked why we had cigarette advertising on the side of our hand-held shopping baskets. He was telling his students about the evil of smoking cigarettes, but when they went into our stores, they saw the endorsement of the product.

The cigarette companies paid us a lot of money to advertise their product on our baskets—enough to make the cost of the hand-held baskets free. But I realized the teacher had a good point. I'm sure many other customers felt the same way but never mentioned it.

So we took cigarette advertising off our baskets. It was the right thing to do, whether one customer or one hundred customers complained.

RULE 45

Monitor your customer service successes and failures.

KEEP TRACK OF the number of positive customer comments as well as the negative. When you do this, you will be keeping your eye on being a superior service provider, and you will continue to improve your service. Each year you should show improvement on your service.

Don't let negative comments get you down—they give you an opportunity to do better. Know the percentage of positive and negative comments on your cards.

Make your goal one hundred percent positive comments. If you don't set a high standard, you won't even reach sixty percent positive.

Be proud of your customer service improvements, but never satisfied.

RULE 46

Make every employee part of the customer service team.

ALL YOUR EMPLOYEES, not just your front-line employees, need to understand your company's commitment to superior service. From the accounting department to the warehouse to shipping, and everywhere in between, every employee must buy into your customer service philosophy.

An employee in accounting told me her neighbor quit shopping with us because she had a problem cashing a check. That afternoon, the store manager went to the neighbor's house to hear about the problem. He gave her a gift certificate and apologized for the treatment she had received when she tried to cash her check.

Later, the accounting employee told me she never realized how serious we were about customer service until she saw what we had done and how fast we reacted to her neighbor's problem. After that, she understood the company's level of commitment to customer service.

For your company to really give superior service, everyone has to be on the same page.

RULE
47

ROI = Return On Individual.

IN ACCOUNTING, ROI stands for "Return on Investment." But I think of ROI as "Return on Individual" instead.

Companies usually see employees as a necessary expense rather than considering their value to the business. Take your profit and divide it by the number of employees you have—that is the Return on Individual.

For example, if your profit at the end of the year is five million dollars and you have two hundred employees, the Return on Individual is $25,000 per employee.

As you grow and add employees, you can do this simple calculation. If you maintain or increase your Return on Individual, you are on the right path.

RULE
48

The CEO must spend time with employees.

THERE IS GREAT truth in the idea of "management by walking around."

It is very easy for the CEO and top management of a large company to get insulated from what is going on in day-to-day operations. They're busy with the management of the big picture, and visiting individual stores to talk with employees can seem too time-consuming. But it's a necessity to run a company that prides itself on excellent customer service. You have to know what the employees are doing, and sometimes you have to see it for yourself.

As president of the company, I visited each of our seventy-two stores unannounced at least once a quarter. I always believed in spending as much time with employees as I could.

When you see an employee do something really well, send a note thanking the employee for how that customer was handled. Let the employee know that this is the kind of service your company really appreciates.

Employees on the front lines can give you valuable ideas about the customer experience in your stores. And employees love the chance to interact with a top executive who's really interested in their opinions about customer service. If management truly listens to the staff, everyone's morale will be improved.

RULE
49

Know the value of a customer.

IN THE SUPERMARKET business, we value a customer at $5,000 a year. If they stay with us for ten years, that's $50,000 worth of business.

Every business can calculate the value of a steady customer. When you teach the value of each customer to your employees, it brings to life how important each and every customer is to the business. Tell employees that when they are confronted with a difficult customer, look at the customer's forehead and imagine a dollar amount written there—the value of that customer to the business. Then make your decision.

Employees will be more responsive to the customer's needs when they know how much each customer is worth to the business.

RULE 50

Serve your community.

WHEN YOU ARE doing business in a community, you need to be a real partner.

When legitimate organizations in your community come to you for a donation, you should give to them. It doesn't always have to be the amount the organization asks for, but you can always give something. It is just what you do as a business leader.

Join the Better Business Bureau and your local Chamber of Commerce. These create relationships in your community.

Choose a local group to support and let your customers know that your business is doing its part. Your reputation will build. People want to shop with community-minded businesses.

RULE 51

Recognize your employees.

IN OUR STORES, we had a "Quiet Hero" award, which was given to employees who went out of their way to do something special for a customer. We used the story of the "Quiet Hero" in our weekly ad.

Our customers knew we were a company that cared about its employees. This public recognition of employees helped build our great reputation in our communities.

RULE 52

Walk the talk.

DON'T JUST GIVE presentations on customer service—set an example.

When I would visit one of our supermarkets, and it was really busy, I would always jump in and help sack groceries.

I liked it—and it was great fun to see the faces of the employees and customers when word got around that "the president of the company is bagging at register number two." It is a powerful way for employees and customers to see that the president is serious about customer service.

You can't just talk customer service. You have to set the example 24/7.

YOU GOTTA KNOW THE Rules!

Animation Rules!
by Steve Hickner

Customer Service Rules!
by Don Gallegos

Business Rules!
by Michael Sansolo

Retail Rules!
by Kevin Coupe

AVAILABLE 2015

Supermarket Rules! Marketing Rules!
Feedback Rules! Customer Experience Rules!

To browse our entire collection of **Rules!** books, visit
www.therulesbooks.com

Also by Don Gallegos

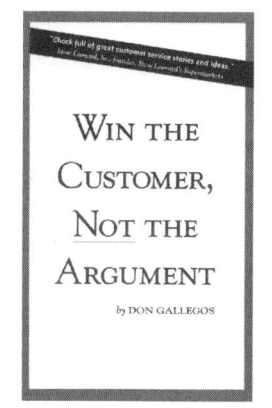

Win the Customer, Not the Argument is a classic book on customer service. Don's philosophy of customer service is "The customer is NOT always right, but he or she is always the customer." Stories, anecdotes, and examples offer hundreds of ideas to make a business more customer-driven.

$14.95
ISBN: 978-0-9711542-4-7
144 pp.

Available at
www.brigantinemedia.com

Made in the USA
San Bernardino, CA
12 September 2014